MARYLAND

The Old Line State

BY
JOHN HAMILTON

Abdo & Daughters

An imprint of Abdo Publishing | abdopublishing.com

abdopublishing.com

Published by ABDO Publishing, a division of ABDO, PO Box 398166, Minneapolis, Minnesota 55439. Copyright © 2017 by Abdo Consulting Group, Inc. International copyrights reserved in all countries. No part of this book may be reproduced in any form without written permission from the publisher. ABDO & Daughters™ is a trademark and logo of ABDO Publishing.

Printed in the United States of America, North Mankato, Minnesota.
022016
092016

Editor: Sue Hamilton   **Contributing Editor:** Bridget O'Brien
Graphic Design: Sue Hamilton
Cover Art Direction: Candice Keimig   **Cover Photo Selection:** Neil Klinepier
Cover Photo: iStock
Interior Images: Alamy, AP, Baltimore Orioles, Baltimore Ravens, Chesapeake Bay Maritime Museum, Chesapeake Bayhawks, Corbis, Dreamstime, Getty, Granger Collection, History in Full Color-Restoration/Colorization, iStock, Jennifer Boyer, Jimmy Emerson, John Bower, Library of Congress, Maryland Historical Society Library, Maryland State Archives, Mile High Maps, New York Public Library, National Archives and Records Administration, U.S. Army Center of Military History, Wikimedia.

Statistics: *State/City Populations*, U.S. Census Bureau, July 1, 2015/2014 estimates; *Land and Water Area*, U.S. Census Bureau, 2010 Census, MAF/TIGER database; *State Temperature Extremes*, NOAA National Climatic Data Center; *Climatology and Average Annual Precipitation*, NOAA National Climatic Data Center, 1980-2015 statewide averages; *State Highest and Lowest Points*, NOAA National Geodetic Survey.

Websites: To learn more about the United States, visit booklinks.abdopublishing.com. These links are routinely monitored and updated to provide the most current information available.

Cataloging-in-Publication Data

Names: Hamilton, John, 1959- author.
Title: Maryland / by John Hamilton.
Description: Minneapolis, MN : Abdo Publishing, [2017] | Series: The United
    States of America | Includes index.
Identifiers: LCCN 2015957612 | ISBN 9781680783223 (lib. bdg.) |
    ISBN 9781680774269 (ebook)
Subjects: LCSH: Maryland--Juvenile literature.
Classification: DDC 975.2--dc23
LC record available at http://lccn.loc.gov/2015957612

CONTENTS

THE OLD LINE STATE

Maryland is a state of contrasts, a mix of North and South. It is sometimes called "America in Miniature." There are sandy Atlantic Ocean beaches and craggy Appalachian Mountains, Chesapeake Bay wetlands and rolling hills of the Piedmont Plateau, sleepy farm towns and bustling cities. Maryland is a snapshot of the entire country rolled into a single, compact state.

Early in its history, Maryland became wealthy because of agriculture, fishing, and trade. Today, a mix of industries combine to give the state a strong economy. Many Marylanders are involved in manufacturing, high-technology businesses, or government services.

Maryland's nickname is "The Old Line State." It honors the brave Maryland soldiers who stood their ground at the Battle of Long Island during the American Revolution.

Maryland has a long history of brave military service to the United States. The Antietam National Battlefield honors the thousands who died during the bloodiest battle of the Civil War.

Two ships sail off the coast of Chestertown, Maryland.

QUICK FACTS

Name: Maryland is named after Queen Henrietta Maria (1609-1669). She was the wife of England's King Charles I (1600-1649).

State Capital: Annapolis, population 38,856

Date of Statehood: April 28, 1788 (7th state)

Population: 6,006,401 (19th-most populous state)

Area (Total Land and Water): 12,406 square miles (32,131 sq km), 42nd-largest state

Largest City: Baltimore, population 622,793

Nickname: The Old Line State

Motto: *Fatti Maschii, Parole Femine* (Manly Deeds, Womanly (gentle) Words)

State Bird: Baltimore Oriole

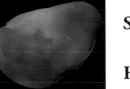

State Flower: Black-Eyed Susan

State Gemstone: Patuxent River Stone (agate)

State Tree: White Oak

State Song: "Maryland, My Maryland"

Highest Point: Hoye-Crest of Backbone Mountain, 3,360 feet (1,024 m)

Lowest Point: Atlantic Ocean, 0 feet (0 m)

Average July High Temperature: 87°F (31°C)

Record High Temperature: 109°F (43°C), in Cumberland and Frederick on July 10, 1936

Average January Low Temperature: 24°F (-4°C)

Record Low Temperature: -40°F (-40°C), in Oakland on January 13, 1912

Average Annual Precipitation: 44 inches (112 cm)

Number of U.S. Senators: 2

Number of U.S. Representatives: 8

U.S. Postal Service Abbreviation: MD

GEOGRAPHY

Maryland is in the Mid-Atlantic region of the United States. Its total land and water area is 12,406 square miles (32,131 sq km). That makes it the 42nd-largest state. It shares a long northern border with Pennsylvania. (The border is called the Mason-Dixon Line.) To the east is Delaware. Two states, West Virginia and Virginia, are Maryland's neighbors to the south. Tucked into a corner of the state's southwest is Washington, DC. The nation's capital rests on a piece of land donated by Maryland in 1790.

Maryland has many kinds of land, which is why it is called "America in Miniature." There are three main regions. They include the Appalachian Mountains in the west, the Piedmont Plateau in central Maryland, and the Coastal Plain in the east.

Catoctin Mountain Park

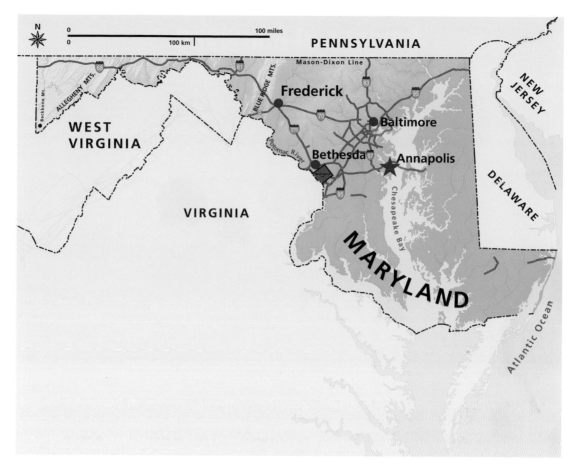

Maryland's total land and water area is 12,406 square miles (32,131 sq km). It is the 42nd-largest state. The state capital is Annapolis.

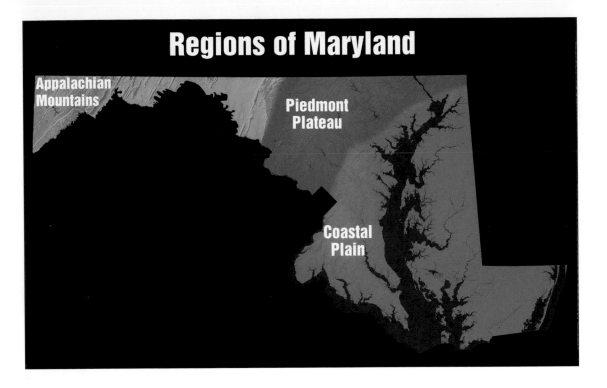

Regions of Maryland

The Coastal Plain is Maryland's largest region. It covers more than half the state. Its eastern edge touches the Atlantic Ocean. The region is mostly flat, with many streams, rivers, and marshes. There is also much fertile farmland.

In the middle of the Coastal Plain is Chesapeake Bay. It is about 200 miles (322 km) long, running roughly north and south. It is the largest estuary in the country. An estuary is a body of water where saltwater from the sea and fresh water from rivers meet. The bay divides the Coastal Plain into the Western Shore and the Eastern Shore. The Eastern Shore rests on the Delmarva Peninsula, which Maryland shares with Delaware and Virginia.

The Piedmont Plateau is in central Maryland. As part of the foothills of the Appalachian Mountains, it is a region with gently rolling hills, forests, and fertile valleys.

Maryland's western panhandle is the forested Appalachian Mountains region. The Blue Ridge and Allegheny Mountains are parts of the Appalachian Mountains. Between mountain ranges are a series of ridges and valleys. The state's highest point is in the far western part of this region. It is Hoye-Crest of Backbone Mountain, which rises up 3,360 feet (1,024 m).

Maryland's most important rivers are the Potomac, Susquehanna, and Patuxent Rivers. The Chesapeake and Delaware Canal cuts across the northeastern part of the state and through Delaware until it reaches the Delaware River. The 14-mile (23-km) -long canal makes it easier for cargo ships from Baltimore, Maryland, to reach the Atlantic Ocean or Philadelphia, Pennsylvania.

The Potomac River creates a border between Maryland and Virginia.

CLIMATE AND
WEATHER

Maryland's three regions have dramatically different climates. The Coastal Plain has a humid climate. The weather is usually mild, but temperatures can dip in the winter months. For the most part, temperatures are steady thanks to the influence of Chesapeake Bay and the Atlantic Ocean.

Inland Maryland, in the Appalachian Mountains and Piedmont Plateau regions, has considerable temperature swings. Temperatures can range from well over 100°F (38°C) in the summer, to far below 0°F (-18°C) in winter in the mountains of the western panhandle.

People ski on a city street during a snowstorm in Frederick, Maryland.

Maryland's record high temperature was 109°F (43°C) in the towns of Cumberland and Frederick on July 10, 1936. The record low sank to -40°F (-40°C) in the mountain town of Oakland on January 13, 1912.

Maryland gets the most precipitation in July and August, when summer thunderstorms rumble overhead. The state is drier in winter. The driest areas are the ridges and valleys of the western part of the state. Maryland's average annual precipitation is 44 inches (112 cm).

Heavy winds and rain send people running near Ocean City, Maryland.

PLANTS AND ANIMALS

Forests make up about 40 percent of Maryland's land area. That is 2.4 million acres (971,246 ha). There are more than 160 kinds of trees in the state. At least 60 are native to Maryland. Oak and hickory are the most common hardwoods. They represent about 60 percent of forestlands. The most common softwood is loblolly pine. It is most often found on the Eastern Shore of Chesapeake Bay.

Other trees found in Maryland include bald cypress, gum, hickory, walnut, poplar, maple, beech, and birch. Maryland's official state tree is the white oak. Some white oaks can live for hundreds of years. They have massive trunks and can reach heights up to 100 feet (30 m). Their acorns are valuable food for forest animals.

There are approximately 15 kinds of bay grasses found in Chesapeake Bay. Bay grasses live underwater in tidal waters. They help improve water quality and give food and shelter to fish and waterfowl. They also help prevent shore erosion.

Many kinds of wildflowers bloom in Maryland, including primrose, spiderwort, iris, goldenrod, and wild blue indigo. The official state flower is the black-eyed Susan.

Wild Blue Indigo

Black-Eyed Susan

Blue Crab in Eel Grass

PLANTS AND ANIMALS

White-tailed deer are found in abundance throughout Maryland. They are especially common in forested mountain areas. Sika deer are native to Asia, but have been introduced to the marshes and wetland forests surrounding Chesapeake Bay. They have chestnut brown coats with white spots.

Other common Maryland mammals include opossums, eastern cottontails, gray and red foxes, coyotes, eastern chipmunks, groundhogs, eastern gray squirrels, southern flying squirrels, beavers, striped skunks, raccoons, muskrats, and brown bats. Wild Chincoteague ponies are found on Assateague Island. They are descended from horses turned loose on the island more than 400 years ago.

A wild Chincoteague pony on Assateague Island, Maryland.

Many kinds of Maryland songbirds can be seen flying overhead or perched on tree branches. They include bluebirds, cardinals, and robins. Maryland's official state bird is the Baltimore oriole. Adult males sport an unmistakable bright orange coloring on their undersides. Other Maryland birds include doves, hawks, hummingbirds, and owls. Nesting in the state's wetland areas are eagles, herons, geese, osprey, and swans.

Baltimore Oriole

Maryland has 27 species of snakes slithering underfoot. Only two are poisonous. They include copperheads and timber rattlesnakes.

Maryland's rivers and coastal waters are teeming with life. Common fish include trout, bass, bluegill, carp, tuna, yellow perch, catfish, herring, shad, red drum, white marlin, northern pike, and walleye. Shellfish are harvested by the ton from Chesapeake Bay. They include blue crab, oysters, scallops, and clams.

PLANTS AND ANIMALS

HISTORY

People have been living in the Maryland area for thousands of years. About 12,000 years ago, as the last Ice Age glaciers melted, Paleo-Indians arrived. They were the ancestors of today's Native Americans. They hunted animals with stone spear points. Later, they learned to gather oysters. In time, they began to gather in villages. In addition to hunting and fishing, they grew crops such as corn, peas, squash, and tobacco. They also made pottery.

By the time the first Europeans arrived in the 1600s, there were many Native American tribes in Maryland. Most were Algonquian-speaking people. They included the Accohannock, Assateague, Delaware, Matapeake, Choptank, Piscataway, Nanticoke, Pocomoke, and Shawnee tribes.

Early Native Americans fished in the Chesapeake Bay area.

John Smith was an explorer from England. In 1608, he sailed his ship into Chesapeake Bay and mapped the area. In 1632, King Charles I of England granted permission to settle a colony on the land. The first governor was Leonard Calvert. The colony was named Maryland to honor the king's wife, Queen Henrietta Maria.

The colonists set up trading posts and began farming the land. Their number-one cash crop was tobacco. Convicts, indentured servants, and African slaves were forced to help with the harvest.

On March 25, 1634, Leonard Calvert led British colonists to a settlement in Maryland. Today, the date is celebrated as "Maryland Day."

Maryland was founded in part by Roman Catholics who fled England. They were escaping legal trouble from England's Protestant-led government. In 1649, the colonists passed the Maryland Toleration Act. It gave rights to all Christians. It was the first law in British North America that guaranteed religious freedom.

In 1694, the Maryland government moved the colonial capital to the city of Annapolis. It was a busy port city, which contributed to its wealth. It was also a slave trade center. Large farms called plantations grew tobacco in southern Maryland. The plantation owners made fortunes by forcing African slaves to work the fields.

From 1763 to 1767, Charles Mason and Jeremiah Dixon surveyed Maryland's northern boundary with Pennsylvania. The boundary became known as the Mason-Dixon Line. It divided slave states from free states during the 1800s until the Civil War.

From 1763 to 1767, Charles Mason and Jeremiah Dixon surveyed the boundary line between Maryland and Pennsylvania. This became known as the Mason-Dixon Line.

On March 15, 1781, during the Battle of Guilford Courthouse, the 1st Maryland Regiment conducted a fierce attack and bayonet charge against experienced British troops. The brave Maryland soldiers impressed their American generals, including Nathanael Greene and George Washington.

During the 1760s, wheat and flour mills boosted Maryland's economy. The shipbuilding industry also grew. Baltimore became a huge center of trade. From the city's port, goods could be shipped almost anywhere in the world.

In 1775, Maryland joined 12 other colonies in the fight for independence from Great Britain during the American Revolution (1775-1783). There were no major battles in the colony. However, Maryland soldiers, known as the Maryland Line, impressed General George Washington with their bravery. This led to Maryland's nickname: The Old Line State.

After winning independence from Great Britain, the American colonies formed a new government. On April 28, 1788, Maryland ratified (approved) the United States Constitution and became the seventh state to join the Union.

During the War of 1812 (1812-1815), British forces bombarded Fort McHenry in the port city of Baltimore. The

In September 1814, Patriot Francis Scott Key was held on a British ship in Baltimore Harbor. After witnessing the attack on Fort McHenry and the American flag continuing to wave, Key was inspired to write "The Star-Spangled Banner."

attack failed. The battle inspired Maryland native Francis Scott Key to write "The Star-Spangled Banner." It became the United States' national anthem.

After the war, new roads and railroads made it easier to move farm products and factory goods. Tobacco continued to be a major cash crop. However, resistance to slavery grew.

During the Civil War (1861-1865), Maryland stayed in the Union. Most other Southern slave states seceded and formed the Confederate States of America. The war divided Maryland. Most people fought for the Union, but many fought for the Confederates. At Sharpsburg, Maryland, more than 23,000 soldiers were killed or wounded in 1862 at the bloody Battle of Antietam. In 1864, Maryland finally abolished slavery. After the Civil War, the slaves were free, but racial wounds were slow to heal.

Maryland's economy gained strength after the Civil War. In the 1900s, more factories sprang up, and the state became a center of transportation, led by the port of Baltimore. By the early 2000s, Maryland had grown into a strong, diverse state with highly educated workers.

The Union and Confederate armies met at the small town of Sharpsburg, Maryland, near Antietam Creek. On September 17, 1862, they fought the Battle of Antietam. It became the bloodiest one-day battle of the Civil War.

DID YOU KNOW?

- In 1790, Maryland donated land along the Potomac River to establish the new nation's capital of Washington, DC. The city was named in honor of President George Washington. Virginia also gave up land across the river. The total amount of donated land was exactly 100 square miles (259 sq km). Virginia's land was returned to the state in 1846.

- The National Road helped people settle the Ohio River Valley and the Midwest. Construction began in Cumberland, Maryland, in 1811. It was the first highway built with federal money. The United States Congress voted to build it in 1806. By 1818, the road had been completed to Wheeling, in today's West Virginia. By the 1830s, it stretched all the way to Illinois.

- The United States Naval Academy is located in Annapolis, Maryland. It is a four-year school where young men and women learn to become officers in the U.S. Navy and Marine Corps. Nicknamed "The Yard," the academy was founded in 1845. Students are called midshipmen. In a crypt beneath the academy's chapel lie the remains of naval hero John Paul Jones.

- Some historians argue that Maryland's John Hanson (1721-1783) was the first president of the United States. In 1781, Hanson was elected president of the Continental Congress. After winning independence from Great Britain, the nation's first government included a group of lawmakers (the Continental Congress) who were elected from the 13 colonies. The colonies followed a set of laws called the Articles of Confederation. John Hanson was the first person elected under this system to serve a full one-year term. In 1789, the United States Constitution replaced the Articles of Confederation. George Washington was elected as the first president under this new set of laws, which we still follow today.

- Lacrosse is the official *team* sport of Maryland, but the state's official sport is more unusual: jousting. The sport has been popular in Maryland since colonial times. As in medieval tournaments, today's competitors are referred to as knights and maids. Many dress in costume. More than a dozen tournaments are held in the summer months all over the state. Competitors gallop under several arches on an 80-yard (73-m) course and attempt to spear rings that dangle several feet off the ground. The more skilled the jouster, the smaller the diameter of the rings. The smallest ring is just .25 inch (.6 cm) in diameter for professional jousters. The Maryland legislature made jousting the state's official sport in 1962. The Maryland Jousting Tournament Association holds a championship tournament each autumn.

PEOPLE

Frederick Douglass (1818-1895) was born a slave on a Maryland plantation, on the Eastern Shore region of Chesapeake Bay. He learned to read, saying later that "knowledge is the pathway from slavery to freedom." In 1938, he escaped from the plantation and fled to New York City, New York. Douglass became a writer and lecturer, telling people about the evils of slavery. His work demolished the racist idea that African Americans were not as intelligent as whites. His autobiography, *Narrative of the Life of Frederick Douglass, An American Slave,* was published in 1845. It became a best-selling classic of American literature.

Jim Henson (1936-1990) was a puppeteer, inventor, and television producer. He is most famous for creating *The Muppets*, and for his puppeteering work on *Sesame Street*. His most beloved creations included Kermit the Frog, Miss Piggy, Big Bird, and Cookie Monster. Henson won many awards for his work, including several Grammy and Emmy Awards. Henson was born in Mississippi, but grew up and attended college in Maryland.

Thurgood Marshall (1908-1993) was the first African American United States Supreme Court justice. He was nominated for the job by President Lyndon Johnson in 1967. Before serving on the Supreme Court, he was a lawyer. He successfully argued in 1954 before the Supreme Court that having separate schools for African Americans and white children violated the United States Constitution. Marshall was born in Baltimore, Maryland.

George Herman "Babe" Ruth Jr. (1895-1948) was one of the most famous professional baseball players of all time. He started his 22-season career with the Baltimore Orioles and the Boston Red Sox, but he is most famous as a slugger for the New York Yankees. He played with the team from 1920-1934. He held a lifetime record of 714 home runs. "The Bambino" was one of the first five players chosen in 1936 for the National Baseball Hall of Fame in Cooperstown, New York. Ruth was born in Baltimore, Maryland.

Edgar Allan Poe (1809-1849) was an author whose books and poems explored themes of death and dread. His best-selling poems, short stories, and books made him a great figure in American literature. His most popular works included "The Raven," "The Fall of the House of Usher," and "The Pit and the Pendulum." He also wrote some of the earliest detective and science fiction stories. Poe spent much of his adult life in Baltimore, Maryland.

Harriet Tubman (c. 1820-1913) was an abolitionist who used the Underground Railroad to lead slaves to freedom. Born a slave in Maryland, she escaped in 1849 and fled to Philadelphia, Pennsylvania. She returned to Maryland many times, helping hundreds of slaves escape to northern states and Canada. Rewards were offered for her capture. During the Civil War, she was a nurse and a scout for the Union army. After the war, she set up care centers to help newly freed African Americans.

Michael Phelps (1985-) is a world-record-holding swimmer who has more Olympic medals than any other athlete. He won 22 medals (18 gold, 2 silver, 2 bronze) in three Summer Olympic Games, including Athens, Greece; Beijing, China; and London, Great Britain. *Sports Illustrated* named him Sportsman of the Year in 2008. Phelps was born and grew up in Baltimore, Maryland.

CITIES

Baltimore is Maryland's largest city. Its population is 622,793. Founded in 1729, it is a city full of history, with many important buildings and monuments. There are also modern high-rises that are home to service-industry businesses such as banking and insurance. The city's top two employers are world-famous Johns Hopkins Hospital and Johns Hopkins University. Located near Chesapeake Bay, Baltimore has one of the busiest seaports on the East Coast. Tourism brings millions of visitors to the city each year. The historic Inner Harbor waterfront district has many attractions, including the National Aquarium. Other popular destinations include Fort McHenry, the Walters Art Museum, the Babe Ruth Birthplace and Museum, and the Baltimore Museum of Industry.

The port city of **Annapolis** has been Maryland's state capital since 1694. Its population is 38,856. It is located where the Severn River empties into Chesapeake Bay, just 30 miles (48 km) east of Washington, DC. Annapolis also served as the nation's capital from 1783 to 1784. It was once a port for the slave trade. Today, it is a major center for boating. Its nickname is "America's Sailing Capital." Tourism is a big part of the city's economy. Visitors like seeing the many preserved colonial buildings from the 1600s and 1700s. Major employers include government services, health care, telecommunications, and retail. Annapolis is the home of the United States Naval Academy.

CITIES

Bethesda is a Maryland suburb of Washington, DC. It is located northwest of the nation's capital. Its population is 63,374. Its residents are well educated and wealthy. It has quiet neighborhoods and a downtown filled with restaurants, theaters, art galleries, and shops. The main campus of the National Institutes of Health is in the city. It conducts research on diseases and public health. Walter Reed National Military Medical Center is a top military hospital. Many United States presidents have received care at Walter Reed. Other major employers in Bethesda include the Consumer Product Safety Commission, Lockheed Martin, Marriott International, and Coventry Health Care.

Frederick was founded in 1745. Located in north-central Maryland, it has long been a crossroads city. It is a north-south gateway, and a link between eastern Maryland and the mountains of the west. Both Union and Confederate armies marched through Frederick during the Civil War. Today, the city's population is 68,400. Fort Detrick, a United States Army bio-medical research center, is Frederick's number-one employer. Other important industries include education, health care, government services, and insurance. With its many historic churches, Frederick is often called the "City of Clustered Spires." Camp David, the country retreat for United States presidents, is just north of the city.

TRANSPORTATION

There are about 32,422 miles (52,178 km) of public roadways in Maryland. For passenger cars and trucks, there is a large system of interstate and state highways that crisscross the state. There are more than 2,500 bridges in Maryland. The Chesapeake Bay Bridge is one of the world's longest. It spans 4.3 miles (6.9 km) across Chesapeake Bay. About 25.6 million vehicles cross the bridge each year.

The deepwater Port of Baltimore is a major freight-shipping center. It is one of the busiest ports in the nation, handling nearly 30 million tons (27 million metric tons) of foreign cargo each year. It supports thousands of jobs in the area. The port also handles large cruise ships.

Norfolk Southern and CSX are the two main freight railroads in Maryland. The biggest rail yards are in Baltimore and Cumberland. Maryland has an extensive passenger rail system that whisks commuters across the busy Baltimore and Washington, DC, metropolitan corridor. Baltimore's Penn Station serves more than one million passengers yearly.

Maryland has more than 200 airports. The busiest is Baltimore Washington International Thurgood Marshall Airport. Almost 23 million passengers fly into and out of the airport each year.

Chesapeake Bay Bridge, commonly called "Bay Bridge," connects the Eastern and Western Shores of Maryland.

NATURAL
RESOURCES

There are more than 12,000 farms in Maryland, with an average size of 165 acres (67 ha). The market value of all farm products sold is more than $2 billion yearly. The most valuable products are eggs and poultry. Corn and soybeans are the most valuable crops grown. Other Maryland farm products include wheat, hay, melons, apples, barley, potatoes, peaches, cucumbers, milk and beef cattle, hogs, and broiler chickens.

A deer peers out of a
Maryland wheat field.

36

Watermen crab near Ridge, Maryland.

Commercial fishing has long been an important part of Maryland's economy. Most fish are taken from Chesapeake Bay, but there are also boats that operate in the Atlantic Ocean. Maryland's blue crabs are a favorite of seafood lovers, especially when steamed and spiced with Old Bay Seasoning. Other undersea catches include oysters, clams, striped bass, yellow perch, and menhaden.

Maryland's forest industry is the fifth-largest industry in the state. It adds about $4 billion to the economy each year, and employs nearly 5,000 people.

In Maryland's western Appalachian Mountains region, hundreds of mines employ nearly 1,300 people. There are about 60 active coal mines in the state, producing more than 2 million tons (1.8 million metric tons) of coal annually. Other minerals dug from Maryland's mines include crushed stone, clay, plus sand and gravel.

NATURAL RESOURCES

INDUSTRY

Maryland is one of the wealthiest states in the country. Even though Baltimore and the Maryland suburbs of Washington, DC, have some poor neighborhoods, the state overall enjoys a very good economy. Unemployment is usually low, especially among the state's highly educated workers. Many Marylanders find jobs working for the federal government in Washington, DC. Others are employed in large, high-technology companies. They produce goods such as software, aerospace equipment, biotechnology, or weapons for the military.

Maryland is a center for health care and life science research. It is home to many world-class hospitals and research centers, including Johns Hopkins Hospital, Bethesda Naval Hospital, the University of Maryland, and the National Institutes of Health.

Baltimore's Johns Hopkins Hospital is one of the top health care systems in the United States.

Manufacturing is another big part of Maryland's economy. The industry is led by chemical, computer and electronics, food and beverage, and plastics manufacturers.

Tourism is very important to Maryland. Each year, about 38 million visitors spend more than $16 billion in the state. Tourism supports more than 140,000 Maryland workers.

Thousands of tourists come to Baltimore's Inner Harbor for events such as Sail Baltimore's visiting ships program. It offers free tours of tall ships and many other vessels.

SPORTS

Maryland has two major league professional sports teams. The Baltimore Ravens play in the National Football League (NFL). The Ravens won the Super Bowl championship for the 2000 and 2012 seasons. The Baltimore Orioles are a Major League Baseball (MLB) team. The Orioles won the World Series title in 1966, 1970, and 1983.

Lacrosse is the official team sport of Maryland. The Chesapeake Bayhawks are a professional lacrosse team based in Annapolis. They won the Steinfeld Cup championship in 2002, 2005, 2010, 2012, and 2013.

The University of Maryland, in College Park, has many athletic teams. Called the Terrapins, or "Terps," they are best known for their basketball team. They won a NCAA national championship in 2002.

The United States Naval Academy in Annapolis has many athletic teams. Their football program has a famous rivalry with the United States Military Academy at West Point, New York. Army-Navy games have been played each year since 1930.

Testudo is the Terrapins' mascot.

Chesapeake Bay is a popular place for sailing and boating.

Marylanders have a reputation for loving outdoor sports. Popular pastimes include backpacking, bicycling, hunting, fishing, camping, golfing, running, and hiking. Along the Atlantic coastline and inland waters, people enjoy parasailing, kayaking, canoeing, and windsurfing. Chesapeake Bay is world famous for boating and sailing.

SPORTS

ENTERTAINMENT

The Baltimore Museum of Art includes more than 95,000 works of art in its collection, including paintings from Henri Matisse, Pablo Picasso, Vincent van Gogh, and Andy Warhol. The Walters Art Museum in Baltimore has collections that include Egyptian mummies, medieval armor, and rare books.

Other Maryland museums include the Chesapeake Bay Maritime Museum in St. Michaels, the Maryland Science Center in Baltimore, the National Museum of Civil War Medicine in Frederick, and the United States Naval Academy Museum in Annapolis. The B&O Railroad Museum in Baltimore has one of the finest collections of historic locomotives in the world.

The Chesapeake Bay Maritime Museum has 12 buildings of exhibits, 12 vessels on floating display at their docks, plus the 1879-built Hooper Strait Light.

The Maryland Zoo has more than 1,500 animals, including giraffes and elephants.

Baltimore's Maryland Zoo is home to more than 1,500 animals representing almost 200 species, including polar bears, lions, giraffes, and elephants. The National Aquarium is also in Baltimore. It houses more than 20,000 aquatic animals.

Classical music lovers can listen to symphony orchestras in Baltimore, Annapolis, Bethesda, and Hagerstown. The Baltimore Symphony Orchestra performs more than 130 concerts each year.

Ocean City, a beach resort town along the Atlantic coast, is home to several amusement parks. Thrill seekers can ride roller coasters and more at Six Flags America in Upper Marlboro, Maryland.

ENTERTAINMENT

TIMELINE

10,000 BC—The first Paleo-Indians enter the land that will become modern Maryland.

1608—John Smith sails his ship into Chesapeake Bay and maps the area.

1632—England's King Charles I grants permission to start a colony. Leonard Calvert is the colony's first governor.

1694—Maryland moves the colonial capital to the city of Annapolis.

1775—The American Revolution begins. Maryland is one of the original 13 colonies that fights for freedom from Great Britain.

1788—Maryland becomes the seventh state in the Union.

1814—During the War of 1812, the British navy fires on Baltimore's Fort McHenry. After witnessing the battle, Maryland native Francis Scott Key writes "The Star-Spangled Banner," which becomes the national anthem of the United States.

1845—The United States Naval Academy is established in Annapolis.

1861—The Civil War begins. Maryland stays in the Union.

1862—Confederate forces are stopped at the Battle of Antietam. It is one of the bloodiest single-day battles of the war.

1864—Maryland ends slavery.

1889—Johns Hopkins Hospital is built in Baltimore, Maryland.

1952—Chesapeake Bay Bridge opens.

2008—Swimmer Michael Phelps, a Maryland native, wins a record eight gold medals at the 2008 Summer Olympic Games in Beijing, China.

2016—Maryland is slammed by a January blizzard nicknamed "Snowzilla." More than 29 inches (74 cm) of snow falls on Baltimore, an all-time record for a single snowstorm in the city.

GLOSSARY

ABOLITIONIST

A person who favors the banning of an activity, such as slavery or the death penalty.

AMERICAN REVOLUTION

The war fought between the American colonies and Great Britain from 1775-1783. It is also known as the War of Independence or the Revolutionary War.

ARTICLES OF CONFEDERATION

The written rules for the first United States government. It was approved by the original 13 colonies in 1781. The Articles of Confederation were replaced by the United States Constitution in 1789.

CONFEDERATE STATES OF AMERICA

A group of 11 Southern states that broke away from the United States during the Civil War, which lasted from 1861 until 1865.

DELMARVA PENINSULA

The Delmarva Peninsula lies between the Atlantic Ocean and Delaware Bay on the east side, and Chesapeake Bay to the west. Its name is short for (Del)aware, (Mar)yland, and (V)irgini(a). All three occupy a portion of the peninsula.

ESTUARY

A body of water where saltwater from the sea and freshwater from rivers meet.

ICE AGE

An Ice Age occurs when Earth's climate causes a major growth of the polar ice caps, continental ice shelves, and glaciers. The ice sheets can be more than one mile (1.6 km) thick.

INDENTURED SERVANT

Poor people sometimes paid for their ship passage to the New World by working for a company or employer for a number of years. Many contracts lasted three to five years. Most indentured servants worked on farms as field laborers. Indentured servants were like slaves, but after their contracts expired, they were freed.

INTERSTATE

Something that exists or is carried between states. The Interstate Highway System is a nationwide network of high-speed roadways that crisscross the United States.

MASON-DIXON LINE

The Mason-Dixon Line is Maryland's northern-most border, which it shares with Pennsylvania. It traditionally marks the separation between North and South. During the Civil War, it divided slave states of the South from the free states of the North.

PANHANDLE

A narrow strip of land that juts out from the rest of the state. Maryland's panhandle is made up of the state's westernmost region.

PENINSULA

Land with water on three sides.

RATIFY

To sign or approve a document, such as a treaty or contract, to make it official.

UNDERGROUND RAILROAD

The Underground Railroad helped African Americans escape from the slave states. It wasn't a real railroad. Instead, it was a secret network of safe houses and connecting routes that led people to freedom.

INDEX